WORLD CUP SOCCER

BY EMILY SCHLESINGER

WH/TE
L/GHTNING
BOOKS®
NONFICTION

Cryptocurrency

Deadly Bites

Digital Worlds

Droids and Robots

Esports

Flight Squads

Olympic Games

Working Dogs

World Cup Soccer

SADDLEBACK
EDUCATIONAL PUBLISHING
www.sdlback.com

Photo credits: page 13: Evgenii Iaroshevskii/Shutterstock.com; page 13: Evgenii Iaroshevskii/Shutterstock.com; page 23: A.RICARDO/Shutterstock.com; page 28: A.RICARDO/Shutterstock.com; page 29: Rui Alexandre Araujo/Shutterstock.com; page 29: Javi Az/Shutterstock.com; page 30: Vlad1988/Shutterstock.com; pages 36/37: Ugis Riba/Shutterstock.com; page 42: Gabriele Maltinti/Getty Images Sport via Getty Images; page 49: Influential Photography/Shutterstock.com; page 51: Kevin C. Cox/Getty Images Sport via Getty Images; page 52: Aubrey Washington/Getty Images Sport via Getty Images; page 53: Al Messerschmidt/Getty Images Sport via Getty Images; page 53: Pedro Vilela/Getty Images Sport; page 55: fifg/Shutterstock.com

ISBN: 978-1-68021-740-7
eBook: 978-1-63078-910-7

Printed in Malaysia

24 23 22 21 20   1 2 3 4 5

Table of Contents

CHAPTER 1
One World, One Event 4

CHAPTER 2
The First World Cup 8

CHAPTER 3
How the World Cup Works 16

CHAPTER 4
World Cup Stars 22

CHAPTER 5
Unpredictable 28

CHAPTER 6
Shock and Scandal 32

CHAPTER 7
Game-Changing Technology 38

CHAPTER 8
U.S. Men in the World Cup 44

CHAPTER 9
The Women's World Cup 48

CHAPTER 10
The Future of the World Cup 54

Glossary 58

1 One World, One Event

It is the most-watched sporting event in the world. Billions of people tune in. Games air in every country. Fans cheer on every continent. This is the World Cup. It is the ultimate soccer championship.

The numbers are impressive. Over 3 billion fans watched in 2010. This was nearly half of all people on Earth. The same thing happened in 2014. A record was set in 2018. That year there were more online viewers than ever before. Over 1 billion people streamed clips.

FAST FACT: People even watch the World Cup in space. In 2018, astronauts streamed games from the International Space Station.

Why do so many watch? The answer may be the appeal of soccer itself. It is the world's most popular sport. Both men and women play. The rules are easy to understand. Each team wants to score goals. Players mostly use their feet. They cannot use their hands. These are the main ideas.

People may speak different languages. Still, they can share a love of soccer. Some call it a universal language. No other sport has spread so easily around the globe.

PLANET SOCCER

A group wanted to find out how many people played soccer. It counted players from around the world. There were about 265 million in 2006. That was 4 percent of the world population at the time. There are reasons the sport is so popular. Soccer does not require special equipment. All players need is a ball to kick. They can play anywhere, in any weather. Players can be any size too. It is their agility that matters.

The First World Cup

Americans would say the World Cup is for "soccer." But that is not the sport's official name. The true name is association football. Most of the rest of the world calls it "football."

The sport started in England in the 1800s. Boys played at school. Over time, its popularity grew. British people traveled around the globe. They took soccer with them. It spread to new places. By 1900, much of the world loved the game.

SOCCER OR FOOTBALL?

England's Football Association formed in 1863. It made official rules for the sport. At that time, there were two types of football. One was rugby football. The other was association football. Each type had a nickname. Rugby football was called "rugger." Association football was called "assoccer." This got shortened to "soccer." Association football spread to the U.S. However, Americans already played a sport they called football. This was the version played by the NFL today. Americans called association football by its nickname, "soccer," to avoid confusion.

Teams formed in many countries. They wanted to play each other. Common rules were needed. In 1904, a group got together to make them. It was called FIFA. The group organized the sport worldwide.

FIFA dreamed of holding a world championship. In 1930, it happened. The event was the World Cup. It was first held in Uruguay. This is a small country in South America. Its team was the best in the world. They had won at the past two Olympics. Many teams wanted to play them.

People took the event seriously. Thirteen teams competed. Seven were from South America. Two came from North America. Four traveled from Europe.

Half a million fans watched. Uruguay won. Argentina took second place. The first World Cup was a success.

FAST FACT: FIFA stands for Fédération Internationale de Football Association. Seven European countries started it. Now, nearly every country in the world is a member.

The World Cup Expands

The second World Cup was in 1934. Italy was the host. Teams from 32 countries wanted to play. FIFA only let 16 take part. It held games so teams could qualify. For half a century, this was the rule.

The event became a tradition. Every four years, teams played for the cup. Games only stopped during World War II.

Over time, the World Cup expanded. More continents joined in. This included Asia and Africa. In 1982, 24 teams were allowed. Today there are 32. It has been this way since 1998.

Now, almost every country tries out for a spot. Games have been hosted on five continents. It is a truly global contest. South America and Europe still dominate. They have produced every winner. The rest of the world hopes to change that.

FAST FACT: The original World Cup trophy was called the Jules Rimet Trophy. It was named after the FIFA president during the first World Cup. Brazil got to keep it in 1970 because they had won three World Cups. In 1983, the trophy was stolen. It has never been found.

World Cup Hosts and Winners

YEAR	HOST COUNTRY
1930	Uruguay
1934	Italy
1938	France
1950*	Brazil
1954	Switzerland
1958	Sweden
1962	Chile
1966	England
1970	Mexico
1974	West Germany
1978	Argentina
1982	Spain
1986	Mexico
1990	Italy
1994	United States
1998	France
2002	South Korea and Japan (cohosts)
2006	Germany
2010	South Africa
2014	Brazil
2018	Russia
2022	Qatar
2026	United States, Canada, and Mexico (cohosts

NUMBER OF TEAMS	WINNER
13	Uruguay
16	Italy
15	Italy
13	Uruguay
16	West Germany
16	Brazil
16	Brazil
16	England
16	Brazil
16	West Germany
16	Argentina
24	Italy
24	Argentina
24	West Germany
24	Brazil
32	France
32	Brazil
32	Italy
32	Spain
32	Germany
32	France
32	--
48	--

* The World Cup was not held in 1942 or 1946 due to World War II.

CHAPTER 3

How the World Cup Works

The idea behind the World Cup is simple. Every country can enter a team. These teams compete in *tournaments*. One team wins. It is the world champion of soccer.

WHERE PLAYERS COME FROM

Most players at the World Cup are professionals. They get paid to play on other teams. These teams are called clubs. Famous clubs include Manchester United in England, Real Madrid in Spain, Juventus in Italy, Corinthians in Brazil, and Boca Juniors in Argentina. Clubs play each other in regional leagues. The U.S. and Canada share a professional soccer league called Major League Soccer (MLS). It includes teams such as the LA Galaxy, Seattle Sounders, Toronto FC, and New York Red Bulls.

The final tournament lasts about a month. But the process begins long before that. Qualification is the first stage. This lasts two years. There are only 32 spots available. Hundreds of countries want one. They compete to qualify. Games happen around the world. Nearby teams play each other. Top ones go to the final tournament.

FIFA Confederations

FIFA divides the world into six regions. They call these confederations. Each holds qualifying tournaments. The top teams in each region go to the World Cup.

REGION	CONFEDERATION NAME
Africa	Confédération Africaine de Football (CAF)
Asia and Australia	Asian Football Confederation (AFC)
Europe	Union des Associations Européennes de Football (UEFA)
North and Central America	The Confederation of North, Central America and Caribbean Association Football (CONCACAF)
Oceania	Oceania Football Confederation (OFC)
South America	Confederación Sudamericana de Fútbol (CONMEBOL)

The Final Tournament

Teams have qualified. Now they play for the cup. These games take place in the host country.

Group competition is the first stage. It lasts two weeks. There are eight groups. Each has four teams. They play several matches. One team places first in each group. There is a runner-up too. Both teams go to the next stage. The others are out.

There are 16 teams left. The winner in each group plays the runner-up from another group. This is the first knockout stage. Winners go to the next round. Losing teams are out.

The top eight teams are in the quarterfinal. They play four games. Only the winners move on.

Then the competition is down to four teams. This is the semifinal. There are two games. Winners go to the final.

The final match is the ultimate game. Just two teams compete. One wins the title. They can say they are the best in the world.

FAST FACT: Matches are 90 minutes long. In the knockout stages, games cannot end in a tie. If the score is tied after 90 minutes, 30 minutes of play are added. After that, games that are still tied go to a shoot-out.

Winning the World Cup

ROUND OF 16

QUARTERFINAL

SEMIFINAL

Group 1   Winner

Winner

Group 2   Runner-up

Winner

Group 3   Winner

Winner

Group 4   Runner-up

Winner

Group 5   Winner

Winner

Group 6   Runner-up

Winner

Group 7   Winner

Winner

Group 8   Runner-up

Winner

Wo

After the group competition, 16 teams compete in the knockout stages. Winners go on to the next stage until only two are left. Those teams play in the final match. The winner takes home the World Cup.

ROUND OF 16

QUARTERFINAL

SEMIFINAL

Runner-up / Group 1

Winner

Winner / Group 2

Winner

Runner-up / Group 3

Winner

Winner / Group 4

Winner

Runner-up / Group 5

Winner

Winner / Group 6

Winner

Runner-up / Group 7

Winner

Winner / Group 8

4 World Cup Stars

In 1958, TV changed the World Cup forever. Games aired around the world. Fans everywhere could now watch. This was a first. Players became international stars. One stands out.

Pelé was the first world soccer star. He played for Brazil. It was the 1958 final. At only 17, Pelé scored two goals. Brazil won the World Cup.

His career was just beginning. Pelé won two more World Cups. They were in 1962 and 1970. No other player has won so many. Some call him the greatest player of all time.

HOW PELÉ GOT HIS NICKNAME

Pelé's real name is Edson Arantes do Nascimento. As a kid, he admired a goalkeeper called Bilé. He said this name every time he blocked a kick. Classmates thought he was saying "Pelé." That became his nickname.

A Goal to Remember

Diego Maradona has a special honor. He scored the "goal of the century." This was at the 1986 World Cup.

Maradona played for Argentina. His country had just lost a war with England. Now the countries met on a soccer field.

The incredible play took just ten seconds. Maradona got the ball. He ran 55 yards. Five English players tried to stop him. None could. Then he kicked the ball. It sailed into the net. Argentina won the World Cup.

Other World Cup Icons

In 1958, fans saw a talented goalkeeper. He wore all black. This was Lev Yashin. People called him the Black Spider. Black Panther was another name. He played for the Soviet Union. Yashin became a legend. Some call him the greatest goalkeeper ever.

FAST FACT: Pelé played in 14 World Cup games during his career. In those games, he scored 12 goals overall.

Gerd Müller was a great scorer. He played for West Germany. Fans called him the Bomber. Müller scored ten goals in the 1970 World Cup. Four years later, he made the winning goal in the final match.

It was the 1990 World Cup. Argentina's team was the defending champion. Then a small African nation defeated them. This was Cameroon. Roger Milla was their leading scorer. Cameroon advanced to the quarterfinal. Milla became famous for another reason too. He did a joyful dance after each goal. Many players copied his style.

In 1998, Brazil faced France in the final. They already had four World Cup titles. France had none. A French player scored two goals. His name was Zinedine Zidane. Both goals were headers. Brazil was stunned. The team lost 3–0.

FAST FACT: France's 1998 World Cup win was the country's first. It was special in another way too. Zinedine Zidane's family was from Algeria. A million Algerian immigrants lived in France. Zidane became the new face of the team. This made immigrants proud.

Unpredictable

The 21st century has brought many new stars. People argue over who is best. For years, two players topped lists. One was Cristiano Ronaldo. The other was Lionel Messi. Ronaldo plays for Portugal. Messi is from Argentina.

FAST FACT: Cristiano Ronaldo has played professionally for Manchester United, Real Madrid, and Juventus. Lionel Messi has spent his career playing for FC Barcelona.

Soccer's highest award is the Ballon d'Or. This means "golden ball" in French. It is given every year to the best player. For a whole decade, only Ronaldo and Messi won. They each won five times.

The two men broke records. They got awards. However, one thing was missing. Neither had a World Cup win. Many thought that would change in 2018.

A Year of Surprises

The World Cup is impossible to predict. In 2018, Messi's team was knocked out early. So was Ronaldo's. Another name was on people's lips. It was Luka Modrić. He played for tiny Croatia. Only four million people live there.

Something unusual was happening. Croatia kept winning. They beat one large country after another. First, they beat Argentina. Then it was Russia. Next, they beat England. Croatia made it all the way to the final. There they faced France. If Croatia won, it would be the biggest upset of all time.

But France was ready. They had a rising star too. This was Kylian Mbappé. He was only 19. Mbappé became the second teen to score in a World Cup final. Pelé was the first. France won 4–2.

No one talked about Messi or Ronaldo that day. Mbappé and Modrić were the stars. The World Cup shapes history. It creates new soccer legends.

BREAKING THE STREAK

In December 2018, the Ballon d'Or prize was announced. For the first time in ten years, neither Messi nor Ronaldo won. The award went to Luka Modrić. His World Cup performance stood out.

Shock and Scandal

Thousands of people work together to put on each World Cup. Billions of dollars are spent. Usually, everything goes smoothly. But occasionally there are twists.

Red Card Drama

Stress runs high at games. Players sometimes lose their cool. They might break the rules. Some argue or fight. When this happens, the **referee** can take action. He shows a **red card**. The player has to leave the field. No one can replace him for the rest of the game. His team is left short a player. It is a difficult position to be in. Red cards can change World Cup matches.

David Beckham was a young star. In 1998, he went to his first World Cup. He played for England. His team went up against Argentina. It was a knockout round. The score was tied. All eyes were on Beckham.

Then the star lost his temper. He kicked a player. This got him a red card. Beckham was sent off the field. England lost. Many called it a disaster. Some fans never forgave him.

DRACULA ON THE FIELD

It was the 2014 World Cup. Luis Suárez was playing for Uruguay. He clashed with an opponent. Then he did something unusual. Suárez sank his teeth into the player's shoulder. Fans gasped. The player showed his bite marks. But the referee did not give a red card. Many people were outraged. It was the third time Suárez had bit someone during a match. There was an odd twist. This ref had a nickname. It was Dracula. Some thought he looked like an actor who played the vampire on TV. Fans started calling Suárez "Dracula" too. FIFA suspended him for nine games. He was also banned from all soccer activities for four months.

Red card drama also happened in 2006. Zinedine Zidane seemed unstoppable. He had helped France win one World Cup. Now they were close to a second. It was the final. They were playing Italy. The score was tied. Would France bring home another win?

The pressure was on. Then Zidane got upset. He head-butted another player. This earned him a red card. Soccer's king had to leave the game. It was one of the most shocking moments in a World Cup final. France lost the game.

Money Scandal

Red cards affect games. But one event rattled the whole sport. This was a problem with FIFA itself.

There was a press conference in 2002. FIFA's president was at the mic. A reporter asked a question. "Have you ever taken a bribe?"

The room grew quiet. "No," the president said. But the story did not end there.

BEHIND THE BRIBES

Why would someone bribe a FIFA official? FIFA members cast votes. They make many important decisions. One is where to hold the World Cup. Many countries want this opportunity. It brings in money, jobs, and excitement. Another decision is which companies to hire for services. These contracts can be huge. Some try to bribe FIFA members to vote a certain way.

A FIFA official contacted the reporter. He asked to meet at a building. It had to be late at night. The reporter went. Inside, the official gave him an armful of documents. The papers showed mysterious payments. They looked like bribes.

Later, the reporter got a call. It was the FBI. Agents were working on a case. The reporter could help.

It took years to put the pieces together. In May 2015, police arrested a group of FIFA officials. They were charged with taking $150 million in bribes. More arrests came later.

Restoring Trust

This news shocked fans. The World Cup faced a **crisis**. FIFA could lose people's trust forever. Earning it back would take work.

The group made changes. New rules were put in place. These made it harder to get away with bribes. Different leaders were elected too.

Still, many fans were angry. Their trust in FIFA had been shaken. But their passion for the World Cup remained strong. The event survived.

FAST FACT: Andrew Jennings was the reporter who helped expose the FIFA scandal. He also investigated corruption of the International Olympic Committee in the 1990s.

Game-Changing Technology

Trust is key in every sport. Fans must know a game is fair. Referees can help. They make sure players follow rules. A player may commit a foul. If this happens, the referee can give a penalty.

FAST FACT: Becoming a World Cup referee is difficult. Refs must pass fitness tests. They also train their minds to deal with the stress of games. The best ones study teams to see how they play. Only the top refs work at the World Cup.

The type of penalty depends on the foul. Often it is a free kick for the other team. A foul near the goal could mean a penalty kick. One player gets a shot at the goal. Only the goalkeeper stands in the way. Many times, the player scores. Penalties can make a big difference in soccer.

Referees face great pressure. One call can change a game's outcome. Mistakes are easy to make. Sometimes calls anger fans too. They may accuse refs of **bias**. Being a World Cup ref is not easy.

A New Approach

In 2018, FIFA tried something new. It used VAR. That stands for "video assistant referee." This was a first for the World Cup.

VAR took a team of people. One trained referee led the team. Three others assisted him. None of them went to the games. Instead, they sat in a central control room. It was filled with screens. For each match, 33 cameras sent video. Of these, 12 were slow-motion.

Each play was carefully watched. Sometimes the team spotted problems. They told the referee on the field. He wore a two-way headset. This let him contact the VAR team too. A screen next to the field showed him replays.

The VAR team gave advice. But it could never make the final call. That was still up to the referee on the field.

FAST FACT: During the 2018 World Cup, VAR was used during all 64 games.

VAR in Action

VAR may have changed the 2018 World Cup final. It was 38 minutes into the game. The referee got an alert. A player might have touched the ball with his hand.

After watching the video, the ref gave a penalty. It was against Croatia. France scored. This helped them win.

During that World Cup, VAR reviewed hundreds of plays. FIFA called it a success.

CRITICS OF VAR

Not everyone is a fan of VAR. Some say slow-motion video hides a player's intentions. A handball is an example. Slow-motion video could show a player's hand touching a ball. But that does not mean the player did it on purpose. This can only be seen by watching at normal speed.

43

8 U.S. Men in the World Cup

Some countries are soccer superpowers. Brazil is one. Germany and Italy are others. France often does well. Argentina does too.

One big country has been missing from that group. It is the U.S. Many find this surprising. In other sports, it rules. But it has not been a leader in soccer.

In 2018, the U.S. team did not qualify for the World Cup. This was the first time in over 30 years. They placed fifth among North American teams. Only the top three went to the World Cup. Fans were upset.

Looking for Answers

Many wonder why the U.S. lags in soccer. The country has talent. It has money too. This has been a winning formula in other sports. But it has not worked in soccer.

A DEVASTATING LOSS

The U.S. team lost qualifying matches for the 2018 World Cup to Mexico and Costa Rica. But they had one last chance to advance. All they had to do was beat the tiny island nation of Trinidad and Tobago. The countries seemed unevenly matched. One was a world superpower. The other was a pair of islands in the Caribbean. Nevertheless, the U.S. lost. It was a stunning defeat.

Experts studied the issue. They found that experience plays a big role. Some countries have a long soccer history. Their teams often do better. Playing many international games helps too. Soccer has not been as popular in the U.S. There have been fewer chances to play other countries.

Another problem could be "pay-to-play." Top youth teams in the U.S. charge money. Parents must pay for their kids to play. It can cost thousands. That leaves out kids with less money. The talent pool is smaller. Other countries have free programs. These help them find young talent.

The biggest reason may be other sports. Soccer is the favorite in many places. This is not true in the U.S. American football is much more popular. Basketball and baseball are too. These sports get the best TV slots. They bring in more money. Many top athletes choose to play them. Fewer choose soccer.

The story may be changing, though. There was a recent survey. Americans picked their favorite sport to watch. Few people over 55 chose soccer. Ten times as many young adults did. Young fans will decide soccer's future. The U.S. could become a soccer nation at last.

FAST FACT: The 2026 World Cup will be hosted by the United States, Canada, and Mexico. Holding games in the U.S. is expected to boost Americans' enthusiasm for soccer.

The Women's World Cup

The U.S. men's team has never won a World Cup. But the women's team is another story. They have three World Cup titles. This is more than any other country. The team dominates women's soccer.

Getting Noticed

The first Women's World Cup was in 1991. China hosted. The U.S. women won. They became heroes in China. But few Americans paid attention. Women's soccer was not big yet.

In 1996, the Olympics included women's soccer. It was the first time. The U.S. hosted the games. Americans saw their team win gold. More people started following the sport.

WORTHY OF THE NAME

FIFA was worried that the first Women's World Cup would fail. They did not want to attach the World Cup name to it. Instead, they called it the "M&Ms Cup." Mars, the maker of M&Ms candies, was the corporate sponsor. After the event went well, FIFA changed the name to Women's World Cup.

The U.S. also held the 1999 Women's World Cup. This time, huge crowds watched. Americans got soccer fever. China and the U.S. met in the final. Over 90,000 fans filled the stadium. It was the most ever at a women's game. The U.S. team won their second World Cup.

2015 Success

The 2015 U.S. team was the strongest yet. They made it to the final. There they faced Japan. Over 25 million people tuned in. It was the most-watched soccer game in U.S. history.

The team proved their strength. They won their third World Cup title.

ULTIMATE GOAL RECORD

Abby Wambach was a top scorer for the U.S. women's team. After winning the Women's World Cup in 2015, Wambach retired with a record of 184 international career goals. This is the most of any player in history, male or female, anywhere in the world.

FAST FACT: Scoring three goals in a game is called a hat trick. It has only happened twice in a World Cup final. Geoff Hurst did it for England in 1966. In 2015, Carli Lloyd did it for the U.S.

American Stars

Many players on the U.S. women's team became superstars. They inspired a new generation. More kids wanted to play soccer.

Michelle Akers was there from the start. She played in the team's first-ever game. This was in 1985. In 1991, she scored ten goals at the first Women's World Cup. She led the team to victory again in 1999. Akers got an award in 2000. FIFA named her Women's Player of the Century.

Michelle Akers

Mia Hamm is one of the country's most famous players. She had two World Cup wins. Her career also included two Olympic gold medals. Hamm won the FIFA award for best women's player twice. In 2007, she got into the National Soccer Hall of Fame.

Carli Lloyd was a star in the 2015 Women's World Cup. She was the first woman player to score three goals during a final. It only took her 16 minutes to do it. FIFA named her the best women's player in 2015. Lloyd won in 2016 too.

The Future of the World Cup

Soccer continues to gain fans around the world. As it grows, so does the World Cup. In 2017, FIFA made an announcement. The World Cup will include 48 countries. This starts in 2026.

Many people were thrilled. New teams would have a chance to qualify.

China is one example. Over a billion people live there. Many are huge soccer fans. But China has only made it into the World Cup once. A bigger event could change that.

FAST FACT: In 2018, over a billion people worldwide watched the World Cup final match between France and Croatia.

Africa would also benefit. It has some strong teams. The Middle East does too. Central America is another hot spot. More teams from these places could qualify.

The change could also help the U.S. It might never miss a World Cup again.

GROWING PAINS

Not everyone is happy that more teams will qualify for the 2026 World Cup. Some think there will be too many games. They won't be as special. Some pro players might not join their national teams. More games would mean needing more time off.

New Ways to Watch

Other changes are making the World Cup more exciting to watch. One is 8K technology. This is ultra-HDTV. It was first used in 2018. Fans went to a museum in Brazil. Special screens were set up. These had 33 million pixels. World Cup games aired on them. They almost looked 3D. Many said it was like being there in person. The technology is expected to spread.

Unforgettable

The World Cup will keep changing. A bigger tournament will bring more fans. Technology will improve. It will capture every kick and foul.

But some things will stay the same. On the field, players will give it their all. The best moments will not need recording. They will be **seared** into the memories of all who watch.

Paul Pogba plays for France. It was the 2018 World Cup. His team was in the final. He gave a pep talk. "I want us to be in the memory of all the French people who are watching us," he said. France's win made sure this wish came true. No one forgets the World Cup.

Glossary

bias: a tendency to take one side over another, even if it is unfair

bribe: a gift given to a person in exchange for doing something illegal or dishonest

crisis: a difficult situation

dominate: to be the best at something

foul: an action that breaks the rules in a game

generation: a group of people born and living during the same time

host: a place that provides everything needed for an event

legend: a person famous for doing something well

match: a game or contest

penalty: a punishment given for breaking a rule

predict: to say what will happen in the future

qualify: to win enough games to be included in a final tournament

red card: a card held up by a referee that means a soccer player who broke the rules must leave the game

referee: a person who makes sure players follow the rules

runner-up: a team that comes in second place

sear: to burn

tournament: a series of games in which teams compete for a prize

tradition: a way a group of people does something

universal: known by most people

upset: a game in which the winner is unexpected

OLYMPIC GAMES

The Early Games

Ancient Greeks liked sports. They enjoyed competition too. It is no surprise they created the Games. The event let them show off their strength and speed.

Big Differences

The word *Olympics* comes from Olympia. This was a sacred site in Greece. The first Games were held there. It is hard to say when they began. Early writings suggest 776 BC. Experts think it was probably earlier.

These contests were not like those of today. They honored the Greek god Zeus. There were no teams. Each man competed for himself. People loved watching the event. Crowds were small though. Most who went lived nearby.

FAST FACT: There were four years between each Olympics. The ancient Greeks named this period of time. They called it an Olympiad.

CHAPTER
3

A Revival

It was 1890. Nearly 1,500 years had passed. A French man traveled to England. His name was Pierre de Coubertin. While there, he met a man who loved sports. The man was trying to restart the Games. Coubertin was inspired. He wanted to help.

In 1894, Coubertin held a meeting. People came from nine countries. Everyone agreed the event should come back. This was an important meeting. It was the start of the IOC. That stands for International Olympic Committee.

The Games began again in 1896. Athens hosted. Over 240 men from 14 countries took part. They played nine sports. Some raced bikes. Others swam and wrestled. There were 43 events in all. More than 60,000 fans showed up. The revival was a big success.

STRANGE SPORTS

New sports are added to the Olympics each year. Some are also taken away. Club swinging began with the 1904 Games. A man would twirl a club like a baton. He would earn points for his routine. Pigeon shooting was in the 1920 Games. The winner shot 21 live pigeons. About 300 birds were killed in all. People thought it was too bloody. The event lasted just one year. Today, people shoot clay discs instead. Tug-of-war was once an Olympic sport too.

FAST FACT: The IOC still runs the Games today. It is based in Switzerland. There may be up to 115 members. They are from all over the world.

16

17

CHAPTER
10

Future Games

The Games face several problems. Cities do not want to lose money. Not all athletes play fair. Safety concerns are also growing. Weather is causing trouble too. Many people are looking for solutions. They want to see the event continue.

No Snow, No Games

Snow is needed for winter sports. But Earth is slowly warming. Experts call this climate change. Some cities get less snow now than in the past. It is only getting worse. Soon they may not be able to hold future Games.

One fix is fake snow. It is made by machines. This is expensive. Large amounts are not easy to make. Fake snow is also lower quality. Natural snow is better.

FAST FACT: Experts have many ideas about how to fight climate change. One is for countries to release fewer greenhouse gases. This could help, but it might not be enough.

50

51

WH/TE L/GHTNING

BOOKS®

NONFICTION

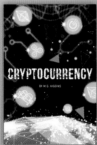

9781680216387

9781680216400

9781680217377

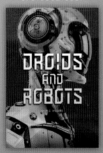

9781680216394

9781680217391

9781680216912

9781680217384

9781680217414

9781680217407

MORE TITLES COMING SOON

SDLBACK.COM/WHITE-LIGHTNING-BOOKS